Skydiving

Skydiving

ROLF BENSON

Lerner Publications Company ■ Minneapolis, Minnesota

ACKNOWLEDGMENTS: All of the photographs in this book have been provided by the author with the exception of the following: pp. 7, 8, 9, 17, 23, Tom VanderVaart; pp. 30, 31, Jerry Irwin and Tom Dunn, United States Parachute Association; p. 33 (bottom), Jim Hovda. The author wishes to give special thanks to Jan Nelson and Kevin Mazzu and to Michael Leeds of *Parachutist* Magazine.

LIBRARY OF CONGRESS CATALOGING IN PUBLICATION DATA

Benson, Rolf.
   Skydiving.

   (Superwheels and Thrill Sports)
   SUMMARY: An introduction to sport parachuting, including training, equipment, skills, and organizations.

   1. Skydiving — Juvenile literature. [1. Skydiving] I. Title. II. Series.

GV770.B46 1979   797.5′6   78-26246
ISBN 0-8225-0425-1

Manufactured in the United States of America. Published simultaneously in Canada by J.M. Dent & Sons (Canada) Ltd., Don Mills, Ontario.

International Standard Book Number: 0-8225-0425-1
Library of Congress Catalog Card Number: 78-26246

1 2 3 4 5 6 7 8 9 10 85 84 83 82 81 80 79

CONTENTS

INTRODUCTION

Human beings have always envied the ability of birds to fly. We have all wondered what it would be like to simply spread our wings and soar. And anyone who has seen films of astronauts has tried to imagine how it would feel to float in the blackness of space.

Ordinary people can achieve the feeling of conquering gravity by taking part in certain sports. Snow skiers thrill as they speed down a slope with the wind tugging at their faces. Water-skiers feel a lake become a solid floor of water that can hold them up because they pass over it so fast. Scuba divers feel weightless as they float beneath the water's surface. Hang glider pilots ride the crest of the wind over sparkling water and through mountain passes.

Skydivers experience *all* these sensations when they jump out of airplanes. They feel the thrills that reward snow skiers, water-skiers, scuba divers, hang glider pilots, and astronauts. That is why skydivers are so enthusiastic about their sport.

Skydiving, or sport parachuting, is done by trained jumpers who delay opening their parachutes after leaving their airplanes. It is during these extended delays that the excitement common to many sports is felt. Try to imagine skiing on a hill that gets steeper and steeper until your skis no longer touch the ground. Or think of standing in a wind so strong that by stretching out your arms, you can leave the ground. Now you

have an idea of how a skydiver feels.

In skydiving, the time you spend falling before your parachute opens is called *freefall*. During freefall you achieve a speed of 120 miles per hour. If you have felt the force of air through an open car window or of water in a fast-moving stream, you can imagine the force of air resistance at such a speed. It feels as solid to the skydiver as water does to a water-skier.

Of course, the air's resistance isn't very useful or much fun unless you can control it. To skydivers, the ability to fall without flopping around is called "falling stable." You fall stable by spreading your arms and legs, arching your back, and keeping your

Skydivers falling together

Falling stable

A skydiver falls through the air.

head back. In this position you will always fall stomach-first, just as you do in a belly flop. From it you can go to freefall maneuvers. By changing the angles at which your body meets the air, you can fall frontwards, backwards, or sideways, go more slowly or faster, turn somersaults and barrel rolls, and even glide a bit like a flying squirrel.

The parachute ride is almost as exciting as the freefall. When you look up and see that big umbrella changing shape like a jellyfish, and then look down and see the patchwork-green landscape, you feel like a hawk or a seagull riding the wind currents. In fact, until you are within 500 feet of the ground, you don't feel as if you are coming down at all.

A skydiver landing

SKYDIVER TRAINING

One of the most basic human fears is the fear of falling. Skydivers must overcome this fear through training and practice. Training teaches skydiving students to know what they have to do and to do it even when they are too frightened to think clearly. For example, when people jump for the first time, they tend to curl up in a ball. This is not a stable falling position. Skydivers must learn the spread-eagle arch so that they will take this position naturally during a skydive. The training they receive also gives them knowledge of safety procedures, a matter of life and death in a sport like skydiving. Skydivers have a relationship to the sky much like sailors have to the sea. The sky and the sea are good friends but are terribly unforgiving of carelessness, neglect, and ignorance. Knowledge and practice on the ground prepare skydivers to make jumps without injuring themselves and without endangering others.

Preliminary training—the basic introduction and ground training—is given by skydiving instructors. These people have had 100 freefall jumps or more and have been involved in the sport for at least two years. They must also have received special training to become licensed and certified as instructors. Skydivers who are qualified to supervise students in the airplane and to review their training are called *jumpmasters*. They must also have had at least 100 freefall jumps and must have received special training in order to become licensed and certified.

During the introduction and ground training, the students learn what they must do to make their first jumps safely. They learn about their equipment—how it works, how to wear it, and how to take care of it. They learn what to do in the plane and how to protect their equipment. They learn how to leave the airplane in a stable falling position. Emergency procedures are learned so that the emergency parachute can be opened safely if needed. Steering the parachute is explained. Students also learn the right way to hit the ground under a parachute in order to avoid broken bones and sprains. Unusual landings—in trees, high-tension wires, or water, for example—are dealt with to insure the students' safety should they occur. Parachute packing may also be taught.

A skydiver practices making a stable
exit from a plane.

After the first few jumps, instruction is given in stability, freefall maneuvers, and spotting. Spotting is the method used to decide when to leave the plane so that the wind will blow the parachute back to the target area. By watching the drift of a weighted crepe paper streamer, the distance and direction of drift can be calculated before the jump is made. On at least the first five jumps, the parachute is opened automatically by the static line, which is attached to the plane. After that, the student opens the parachute. As the lessons continue, the freefall time is gradually increased by 5-second steps to 30 seconds.

A jumpmaster supervises every student jump and makes comments and criticisms in the student's personal log book. Information about every jump a skydiver makes is recorded in this book. The date, the number of the jump, the altitude and freefall time, the type of airplane and equipment used, and the maneuvers performed are all entered.

Learning to release the main parachute is important for safety.

A skydiving student must also know how to open an emergency parachute.

TRAINING EQUIPMENT

The student parachutist's equipment includes a harness, the main parachute, a reserve parachute, helmet, goggles, coveralls, gloves, and boots. The harness is made up of straps that go around the shoulders, legs and chest, thus spreading the force of the parachute opening evenly over the entire body. The straps are connected with snaps so that the harness is easy to put on and take off. They are also adjustable to allow a snug but comfortable fit.

The harness is connected to the parachute lines with releasable clips. These clips let the jumper get away from the main parachute if it isn't working correctly. The clips can also be released if the wind is dragging the jumper after a landing and the parachute can't be deflated by pulling the lines on one side. In the air, getting away from the main parachute lets the emergency or reserve parachute open without tangling in the main. The reserve has a device that automatically opens it if the jumper falls too fast past a certain altitude.

The parachute is made of nylon and is shaped like a big umbrella. Triangular sections of nylon are sewn together with sus—pension lines coming from between the sections. Student parachutes are either 28 or 35 feet in diameter. Several sections are cut out in the back to let air escape. This drives the parachute forward at about five miles per hour. The parachute is steered by pulling lines to close the open section on one side. This allows the other side to push itself around, which turns the parachute in the direction the jumper wants to go.

A helmet protects the jumper's head from the buckles and straps during openings, and from smacking on the ground during landings. Goggles let the jumper see clearly, and gloves prevent rope burns while lines are being handled. Coveralls protect clothes, and boots support the ankles during landings. Care is taken not to wear anything that could snag the parachute.

The prospective skydiver is trained on the ground until the instructor feels the student will be able to leave the plane, steer the chute, handle an emergency, and land. Then the student is fitted with gear and goes on the airplane with a jumpmaster.

A student parachute is designed for an easy descent.

A jumpmaster inspects a student's main parachute pack (*above*) and reserve parachute pack (*below*).

THE FIRST PARACHUTE JUMP

Picture yourself as a student making your very first jump. You carefully protect your gear while the plane climbs to about 2,800 feet. The jumpmaster supervising your jump looks out at the ground and gives the pilot course corrections that will put you over the proper spot. You are told to sit in the door with your feet hanging out. Your heart beats like a bass drum in your throat. The plane is going about 80 miles per hour, the wind is clutching at you, and you are scared. Then the jumpmaster yells, "Get on the step!" You grab the wing strut, pull yourself out, stand with one foot on the plane's tiny step, and let your other foot dangle in the breeze as you look out at clouds and sky. When the jumpmaster yells "Go!" and slaps you on the leg, you simply raise your feet and let go of the strut with your hands, going into the spread-eagle arch. You arch hard with your head back so you can see the plane and the jumpmaster waving at you. As you fall, the static line, which connects your parachute to the plane, automatically pulls out the chute. Within three or four seconds you feel the shock of

opening. You look up and see that beautiful parachute. Then you look down, find the landing area, do a few turns, and steer for the target.

At about 200 feet you turn to face into the wind. With legs and feet together, legs slightly bent and hands above your head, you hit the ground and roll to spread the shock over your body. If the wind drags you, you spill the air from your parachute by pulling in the lines on one side or by releasing a shoulder clip. Then you wind up the lines and canopy and take them to the packing area to be repacked.

During training, you receive packing lessons and supervision until you are capable of packing your own main parachute safely. Before the parachute is repacked, it is stretched out, inspected for tears and broken lines, and folded. A cloth tube, called the *sleeve*, is pulled over the entire length of the folded nylon part of the chute. It slows the parachute opening to about three seconds by keeping the canopy closed until all the lines have come out and are tight. This makes the opening softer and easier on the jumpers and the equipment. Before sleeves were used, the sudden opening often meant bruises for the parachutist. The lines are folded and held in rubber bands at the bottom of the sleeve. Then everything is folded into the backpack.

The folded parachute, pilot chute, and backpack must be carefully inspected before each jump.

A small parachute with a spring in it, called the *pilot chute*, is compressed and put on top of the folded main. Then the flaps of the backpack are wrapped around the entire package and secured by pins attached to a wire. This wire is the *ripcord*.

When you pull the ripcord, it pulls the pins out, the backpack flaps fall open, and the pilot chute springs out into the wind, pulling the main parachute out with it. For the first few jumps, when the opening is automatic, the ripcord is replaced by the static line.

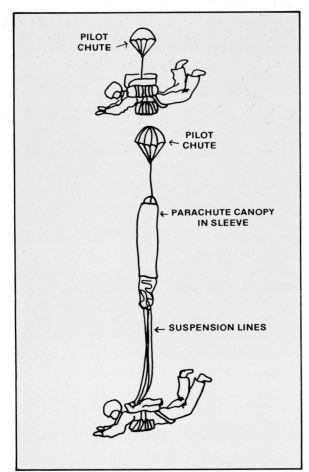

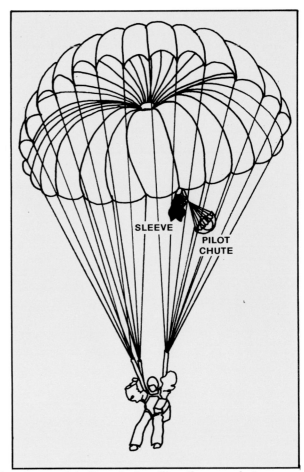

When the skydiver pulls the ripcord, the pilot chute pops up into the wind, pulling the parachute and its lines behind it. The parachute doesn't open until all of the suspension lines are pulled tight.

Parachutes must be inspected after every jump.

DEVELOPING FREEFALL SKILLS

On your first five jumps, you use a static line. After that, the jumpmaster may let you use a ripcord to open the parachute yourself. If you do this well without losing stability by rolling over or flipping, the jumpmaster lets you freefall longer. With each jump, your freefall time is increased. The jumpmaster will begin to tell you how to turn, somersault, roll over, and return to a stable position for the opening. For longer freefalls, the plane must fly higher, so that your parachute will always open at 2,500 feet. The length of the freefall therefore depends upon the height at which the jump begins. The first jumps are freefalls of about 3 seconds, beginning at 3,000 feet. Freefalls of 5 seconds start at 3,200 feet; 10 seconds, at 3,600 feet; 15 seconds, at 4,500 feet; 20 seconds, at 5,500 feet; 30 seconds, at 7,200 feet; 45 seconds, at 10,500 feet; and 60 seconds at 12,500 feet.

A skydiving altimeter tells a jumper when to open the parachute.

When you jump, you wear on your wrist an instrument that shows how high you are above the ground. This is the *altimeter*. When it reads 2,500 feet, you pull the ripcord. By pulling then, you have time to handle any emergency that might occur.

By the time you have had 25 to 30 free-falls and have done 30- and 45-second delays, you start to feel that you know what skydiving is all about. But you are really just beginning. On one of those longer delays your jumpmaster will follow you out of the airplane. While you watch, the jumpmaster will swoop down, stop about 10 feet away, glide slowly in, and grab your arms. Then you'll watch the jumpmaster turn around, fly away very fast, and open his or her parachute. Afterward, you'll think that was one of the most amazing things you've ever seen. There was your jumpmaster, hovering near you like some kind of hummingbird, as if neither one of you were falling at 120 miles per hour. Later you'll realize that while your jumpmaster was free-falling with you, you didn't feel that you were falling at all. You felt as if you were flying. Suddenly you know that it was worth all the work and effort it took to get to this point, and you want to do more.

A jumpmaster joins a student in freefall.

PARACHUTING LICENSES AND AWARDS

Once you have made at least 25 freefalls and have mastered spotting, you can take a written examination for an "A" license. When you have that license, you no longer need a jumpmaster's supervision. Any licensed jumper can sign your logbook. You can jump with other skydivers and polish your skills in landing on the target, maneuvering, and hooking up with others during freefall.

After about 50 jumps you can apply for a "B" license. With 105 jumps or more you can test for a "C" license. The "C" license allows you to jump in public exhibitions. You can also train to become a jumpmaster and an instructor after you have been a jumpmaster for a year. You become eligible for a "D" license after 200 freefalls. The licenses are administered by the United States Parachute Association (USPA).

The USPA is based in Washington, D.C., and has over 15,000 members. It helps regulate the sport, establishes safety standards, sponsors competition events, and provides insurance coverage for its members. It also publishes a monthly magazine, *Parachutist.*

Some people are trained to work with parachutes and parachuting equipment. They are called *riggers.* They are certified by the Federal Aviation Agency, and they are the only ones who should repair or alter equipment. Riggers are also the only people allowed to pack reserve parachutes. Reserve parachutes have to be opened, spread out, and repacked periodically. All parachute equipment is made according to designs that the Federal Aviation Agency has tested and approved.

In addition to the licenses, awards are given to persons completing higher numbers of jumps. Gold wings are given for 1,000 freefalls, diamond wings for 2,000, and double diamond wings for 3,000 freefalls jumps. Some people who have been skydiving for a long time have more than 4,000 freefalls. Award pins are also given for 12 and 24 cumulative hours of freefall time.

FREEFALL MANEUVERS

As we learned earlier, freefall is the time a skydiver spends dropping through the air before opening the parachute. It takes about 1,000 feet of freefall to reach a constant speed, at which the air's resistance equals the pull of gravity. This constant speed is called *terminal velocity*. Falling speed becomes constant between 90 and 120 miles per hour, depending upon the jumper's weight, size, and equipment.

A skydiver in freefall feels the air push very hard against the body and finds that different body positions can be used to change the speed and direction of the fall. This maneuverability is important because it allows skydivers to perform acrobatics and to fly in formations with each other. It lets them leave a plane at different times and join together to create a pattern. They can even jump from different planes and then fly into formations. When the time comes to open their parachutes, the skydivers can maneuver to separate and get clear of each other so they do not collide.

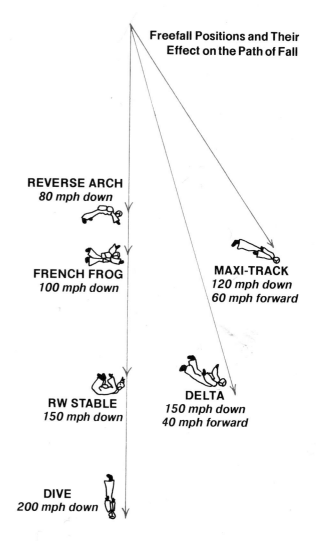

Freefall Positions and Their Effect on the Path of Fall

REVERSE ARCH
80 mph down

FRENCH FROG
100 mph down

MAXI-TRACK
120 mph down
60 mph forward

RW STABLE
150 mph down

DELTA
150 mph down
40 mph forward

DIVE
200 mph down

THE BASIC STABLE SPREAD POSITION

THE RELATIVE WORK STABLE POSITION

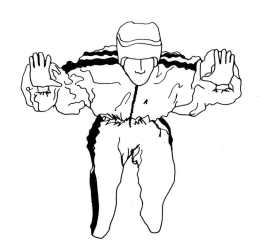

THE FRENCH FROG POSITION

All freefall maneuvers begin with the basic stable spread that students learn. French pioneers in freefall modified this position to the *French frog*, which is more relaxed. This serves the purpose of a stable position. It has a relatively slow falling speed and a vertical path of fall. To increase the falling speed the skydiver can arch the

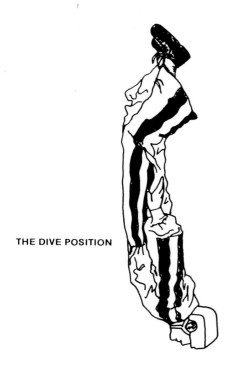

THE DIVE POSITION

THE DELTA POSITION

back very hard and bend the arms and legs so they trail behind the back. This is called the *relative work stable* position. Falling speed can be nearly doubled by straightening the body and legs and grabbing the backs of the legs with the hands. This is the *dive*. It puts the jumper in a standing-on-head position, thereby drastically reduc-

ing the body surface the jumper presents to the air.

To achieve higher falling speed along with some forward glide, the legs are straightened and the arms are held back at an angle from the sides of the body. This is called the *delta* position. More forward glide is generated by holding the arms close to the

THE TRACK POSITION

THE MAXI-TRACK POSITION

body, along the sides, and straightening the legs. This is called the *track*. The forward glide results from the body meeting the air at an angle. To get even more forward glide, the skydiver bends forward slightly at the waist and hunches the shoulders. This resembles the position of ski jumpers and is called the *maxi-track*. Skydivers can move horizontally at speeds of more than 60 miles per hour, while falling at more than 100 miles per hour, by using the track and maxi-track positions.

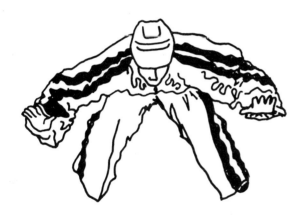

THE REVERSE-ARCH POSITION

To achieve a slower fall, the skydiver's body is bent forward at the waist. The arms and legs are spread wide and held straight but slightly in front so the jumper appears to be draped over a large beach ball. This position produces some instability, but it cups air and slows the rate of fall by 10 to 20 miles per hour. It is called the *reverse arch* and is used only when the skydiver is falling below other jumpers whom he or she would like to join.

Skydivers can turn and flip by moving their limbs and bending their bodies to deflect the air. For example, the skydiver can do a backward somersault by pushing the hands out ahead of the body and tucking the legs into the chest. To stop the somersault, the jumper once again goes into the stable spread position with an arched back. There is a competition event known as *style*, during which jumpers try to complete a series of turns and flips for time.

RELATIVE WORK

Until recent years, skydivers concerned themselves mainly with style and parachute accuracy. Only occasionally did they fly in close formation. In the last five years, however, attention has focused on flying into freefall formations with other skydivers. Such formation flying is called *relative work* (RW) because the jumpers maneuver in relation to one another while in freefall. By using dives, glides, and turns, the jumpers can come together in formations of up to 40 people. This aspect of the sport requires extra training and several hundred jumps to master. However, most skydivers find relative work so fascinating, challenging, and enjoyable that its appeal is almost impossible to resist. In relative work, other jumpers appear to hover and move like bumblebees, and the fact that everyone is falling is almost forgotten. When a day of this kind of jumping is over, hours are spent swapping stories of the jumps and how they looked from each jumper's point of view.

Relative work (RW) is an exciting development in skydiving. Flying into a large relative work formation (*below*) takes skill and practice.

When the last skydiver has flown in, a relative work formation is complete.

Training for relative work begins with two people. One person falls in a basic stable position without sliding sideways, forward, or backward. This person is called the *falling base*. The other skydiver uses a delta position to dive and glide down and over to the base. Just before reaching the base, the second jumper must slow down by pushing against the air with arms and legs spread out. This is called *flaring-out*. The flare-out lets the second jumper glide in slowly and grab the base. They can stay together until they reach 3,500 feet. There they give a signal and turn away from each other. By tracking or maxi-tracking, the jumpers glide apart until they reach 2,500 feet, where they open their parachutes. Before opening, the skydivers must wave their arms and look over their shoulders. This is done to make sure that there is no one above who can fall into an opening parachute.

Gradually, as basic RW techniques are mastered, more skydivers are added. By using larger airplanes, groups of people numbering from 4 to 50 can leave together and perform RW. Several planes can be used with jumpers coming out of each and doing relative work all together. Large-number relative work requires some special techniques because of some special problems. The first problem is getting the jumpers to leave the plane as closely as possible to one another. As many as 3 can hang on outside the door. When these 3 let go, the other jumpers dive head first out the door. In an attempt involving 10 or more people, even this method means there will be four or five seconds between the first and last jumpers.

Aircraft size makes a difference in relative work. A Twin Beechcraft airplane (*above*) can carry approximately 10 skydivers. A DC-3 aircraft (below) can carry approximately 30 skydivers.

Another problem with large number relative work is that a shield of air forms around a formation when three or more people are in it. This shield is called the "burble." A burble will bounce an approaching skydiver away from a formation unless that skydiver has enough speed to penetrate the burble. But if the skydiver has too much speed the entry will scramble the jumpers in the formation. So a jumper must be able to judge exactly what this entry speed should be, and that takes practice and experience.

This experience also helps with a third problem—the sliding a formation may do sideways, toward, or away from approaching skydivers. Corrections in approaches must be made early enough to keep the incoming skydiver from skidding past a formation because it suddenly slides to one side. Also, a formation falls more slowly than a single jumper. A formation of people was once clocked by police radar at a falling speed of less than 80 miles per hour, 40 miles per hour less than the speed of an individual skydiver. So a jumper approaching a formation must take into account that each person entering will slow the formation down.

THE STAR CREST RECIPIENT (SCR) AWARD

THE STAR CREST SOLO (SCS) AWARD

RELATIVE WORK AWARDS

Relative workers can receive two awards that rate their mastery of relative work techniques. These awards are the Star Crest Recipient and the Star Crest Solo awards. The Star Crest Recipient, or SCR award, is given for being one of the first seven people in an eight-person (or larger) round formation that holds for at least five seconds. The Star Crest Solo, or SCS, is given for being eighth or above in a round formation of eight or more. These awards are given by the Bob Buquor Memorial. Bob Buquor was an early skydiver who pioneered large formation relative work. Buquor drowned while parachuting over the ocean in 1965.

35

HIGH PERFORMANCE EQUIPMENT

When relative work started to become popular, people began trying different equipment. Even new types of parachutes were introduced. Until then, everyone had jumped with military surplus gear. Gradually, however, companies were formed to manufacture equipment for sport parachuting. A smaller canopy, with more holes cut in it, was developed and named the *para commander*, or PC. The holes gave it a forward speed of about 12 miles per hour. The parachute could be smaller because lift was created by the air passing over it in the way air passes over an airplane wing. The PC didn't descend any faster than a regular para-

chute but it had more steering ability, which was handy on windy days, and it weighed less. Greater skill was required to use it safely, however, because some maneuvers made it drop very rapidly.

Someone then thought that if a parachute could be shaped just like an airplane wing, almost all the lift could be generated from forward speed instead of from dragging through the air. It was found that such a parachute only had to be one-fourth as big as a regular round parachute. The newly designed parachute had a square outline with the side profile of an airplane wing. It looked something like a big air mattress

Para commander parachutes are designed to give forward speed and greater steering ability.

A jumper turns a square parachute by tilting it.

with the front end cut open to let air force its way inside and inflate the canopy. These parachutes are called *square, flat,* or *ram-air* canopies. They can move forward at speeds up to 30 miles per hour while they come down at the same speed as a regular parachute. They also tilt when they are turned, just as airplanes tilt when they turn. Skill is required to turn these parachutes, however, because turning causes them to suddenly drop faster. This and other characteristics make these canopies dangerous if the jumper doesn't know how to use them. But their advantages outweigh their disadvantages. An experienced skydiver using a square canopy can land softly on one foot even when a 20-mile-per-hour wind is blowing. Coming down under a square is a lot like hang gliding.

Using square parachutes takes skill.

39

Square parachutes can provide more accurate landings than other kinds of chutes.

Another reason for the square parachute's popularity is its compact size. When it is folded, it is so small and light that the square and reserve together weigh less than one military surplus round-type parachute. They will both fit on a jumper's back, so the reserve does not have to be worn on the chest. This makes getting around in the plane and leaving the plane much easier and faster. A jumper in freefall also falls more slowly and can glide forward faster with this type of rig. When both parachutes are worn on the back, the harness assembly is called a "piggyback" or "tandem rig." Modern tandems can weigh less than 25 pounds, while standard student gear weighs nearly 50 pounds. The square's soft landings let jumpers wear low cut tennis shoes and hockey helmets instead of boots and motorcycle helmets. These changes make a sky-diver's equipment weigh even less.

Relative work has also brought about changes in the coveralls skydivers wear. Before, close-fitting coveralls were worn. Then someone tried flappier jumpsuits with bell-bottom legs and sleeves using more cloth. They even added extra material under the arms that looked like a flying squirrel's folds of skin. Cords were sewn into the suit from the waist to the hands so that it could be held tightly in the wind. These new jumpsuits made the jumpers' falls slower and steadier. By wearing this kind of suit and a tandem rig, a jumper can reduce terminal velocity to less than 100 miles per hour instead of the usual 120 miles per hour. This means that freefall can last longer. For example, people have been getting 50-second freefalls from 10,500 feet instead of 45 seconds as before.

SKYDIVING ORGANIZATIONS

Most skydivers either belong to a skydiving club or go to a commercial skydiving center. In a skydiving club the members contribute time and money to operate a jump plane, train students, and maintain facilities. At a commercial center, an individual or a group provides the plane and the facilities for skydivers, who pay anywhere from $5 to $15 for each jump. Commercial operations are designed to make a profit for the operator, while the clubs basically try just to cover their costs. Some skydivers interested in RW form teams and try to jump together as much as possible. Others go to a jump area and jump with any other skydivers who happen to be there. The average jumper makes 3 or 4 jumps on a week-end, but jumpers practicing for competition may make 8 to 10 jumps a day, several days a week. A large airplane that will hold eight or more people will attract skydivers from several hundred miles away.

Skydivers get together in large numbers to jump just for fun, and to compete in meets. The usual events in a meet are landing accuracy, style (one-person acrobatics for time), and relative work. The relative work can be divided into 4-, 8-, 10-, 12-, and 16-person events. Judges watch from the ground while these teams make several formations in a series, working against the clock, or make one formation in the shortest possible time. There are local, regional, and national meets. The national meet is an annual event that last two weeks. Since 1969, annual international competition has also taken place in Yugoslavia, Germany, the United States, and Australia. Skydivers also jump for public exhibitions at air shows, county fairs, and community celebrations. The United States Army's Golden Knights is one famous exhibition jumping team.

Skydiving is a sport that is not suited to everyone. There are age and physical requirements that must be met. A person must have reached the age of 16 and have parental consent before skydiving training can begin. If parental consent is not given, the prospective skydiver must wait until the age of 18 is reached. Every skydiver must carry a statement, signed by a doctor, showing that he or she has passed a physical exam within the past two years. Other requirements and regulations vary from state to state.

Although people become skydivers because they are attracted by excitement and adventure, most skydivers are not daredevils. Because they know the danger involved, skydivers stress safety in training, equipment, and practice. As a sport, skydiving is satisfying because it provides a feeling of accomplishment in overcoming gravity and the basic human fear of falling. The skydiver who trains carefully is rewarded with a sense of belonging to one of the most select groups of adventurers in today's sports world.

GLOSSARY

altimeter—A device that shows skydivers how high they are

burble—A wall of air that trails above a falling body much like the wake of a speed-boat

canopy—The cloth portion of a parachute

delay—The amount of time a jumper waits before pulling the ripcord

delta—A freefall position that produces a higher falling speed and some forward glide. The jumper's arms are held back at an angle from the shoulders and the legs are straightened.

dive—A freefall position that produces very high falling speed. The jumper's arms are held tightly against the sides and the legs are straightened.

emergency (reserve) parachute—A second parachute worn by the jumper for use in case the main parachute doesn't work. It may be worn on the stomach or on the back.

falling base—A jumper who falls in as stable a position as possible to allow others to glide in and hook up during freefall

flare out—Spreading the arms and legs to slow the rate of glide and fall when approaching other jumpers in freefall

freefall—The time spent falling before the parachute opens, during which the skydiver uses the force of air against the body to control movement

French frog—A freefall position originated in France in which the back is arched, the legs are bent at the knee, and the arms are held bent on either side of the head. By using this the jumper's fall will be fairly slow and stable and straight down.

harness—Nylon or canvas straps that fasten around the jumper's body to hold the parachute gear on and spread the shock of the parachute opening evenly over the entire body

instructor—A jumper who trains people to make their first parachute jumps. An instructor has had at least 100 freefalls, has been a jumpmaster for at least a year, and has received special training and certification.

jumpmaster—A skydiver who handles student jumpers in the plane. A jumpmaster has had at least 100 freefalls and has received jumpmaster training.

jumpsuit—Coveralls worn by jumpers. Some jumpsuits have extra material under the arms to give the wearer more control in freefall.

licenses—Certificates administered by the United States Parachute Association for mastery of parachuting skill and knowledge on various levels

logbook—A book for keeping records of each jump a person makes. A logbook is important for students and jumpers applying for licenses or otherwise proving their proficiency and qualifications.

main parachute—The parachute that the jumper originally intends to use. It is generally worn on the back.

maxi track—A freefall position that generates the most forward glide of any position. The top half of the body is cupped forward with the hands at the sides and the legs straight down.

paracommander (PC)—A round-canopy parachute with many holes and slots cut out to redirect the air backwards and generate a forward speed of 12 to 15 miles per hour

pilot chute—A small parachute, sometimes built with a spring inside, which is either thrown or springs into the air and pulls the main or reserve parachute behind it

relative work—Freefall maneuvers done with other jumpers

relative work stable—A freefall position which allows a very fast and straight fall. The back is arched very hard while the arms and legs trail behind the back.

reverse arch—A freefall position which slows the jumper as much as possible. The body is held in a cupped position similar to being draped over a large beach ball.

rigger—A person who is qualified to repair parachutes and pack reserves

ripcord—A metal cable with metal pins on it that holds the parachute pack together until it is pulled to release the parachute

skydiving—Sport parachuting that involves freefall activities

sleeve—A cloth tube that is slid over the canopy during packing to slow the parachute opening and make it more comfortable

spotting—A technique that allows the jumpers to decide when to leave the plane in order to land on target

spread-eagle arch (stable spread)—A freefall position in which the jumper's back is arched and the arms and legs are spread wide. The jumper will then fall forward to earth without flopping around.

square (ram-air, flat) — A parachute that has up to a thirty-mile-per-hour forward speed and comes down like a hanglider. It is shaped a lot like an air mattress.

stability — Freefalling without spinning, rolling over, or otherwise flopping around

static line — A cord connecting the parachute and the plane that opens the parachute as the jumper falls away. It is used by military paratroopers and student skydivers.

Star Crest Recipient (SCR) — A relative work award given to a jumper who was one of the first seven members of at least an eight-person round formation which held stable for five seconds or more

Star Crest Solo (SCS) — A relative work award given to a jumper who has glided in as eighth person or higher in a round formation of eight or more people that has held stable for five or more seconds

style — A freefall activity in which a single jumper performs a series of acrobatics before opening the parachute

tandem — A type of harness which has both the main and reserve parachutes worn on the back

terminal velocity — The maximum speed a jumper will reach while falling in a given freefall position. At this speed the air resistance is equal to the force of gravity on the body.

track — A freefall position that allows forward glide. The back is arched, the legs straightened, and the arms held parallel to the sides of the body.

United States Parachute Association (USPA) — An organization that governs most sport parachuting in the United States. It is based in Washington, D.C., and provides services for its thousands of members. It organizes competition, issues licenses, and publishes a monthly magazine called *Parachutist.*

Superwheels & Thrill Sports

Lerner Publications Company
241 First Avenue North, Minneapolis, Minnesota 55401